The Young Influencer Blueprint 1

The Young Influencer Blueprint

A Momager's Guide To Building Her Child's Personal Brand And Influence

By: Arriel Biggs

ALL RIGHTS RESERVED. No part of this report may be modified or altered in any form whatsoever, electronic, or mechanical, including photocopying, recording, or by any informational storage or retrieval system without express written, dated, and signed permission from the author.

AFFILIATE DISCLAIMER. The short, direct, non-legal version is this: Some of the links in this report may be affiliate links which means that I earn money if you choose to buy from that vendor at some point in the near future. I do not choose which products and services to promote based upon which pay me the most, I choose based upon my decision of which I would recommend to a dear friend. You will never pay more for an item by clicking through my affiliate link, and, in fact, may pay less since I negotiate special offers for my readers that are not available elsewhere.

DISCLAIMER AND/OR LEGAL NOTICES: The information presented herein represents the view of the author as of the date of publication. Because of the rate with which conditions change, the author reserves the right to alter and update his opinion based on the new conditions. The report is for informational purposes only. While every attempt has been made to verify the information provided in this report, neither the author nor his affiliates/partners assume any responsibility for errors, inaccuracies, or omissions. Any slights of people or organizations are unintentional. If advice concerning legal or related matters is needed, the services of a fully qualified professional should be sought. This report is not intended for use as a source of legal or accounting advice. You should be aware of any laws which govern business transactions or other business practices in your country and state. Any reference to any person or business whether living or dead is purely coincidental.

Copyright © Arriel Biggs LLC.
ISBN: 978-1-7374637-4-0
Cover Design: Thornton Online Marketing

Table of Contents

INTRODUCTION	6
LET'S GET STARTED	12
WHAT IS A PERSONAL BRAND?	18
WHY YOU NEED TO BUILD A PERSONAL BRAND	22
Personal Branding Allows You to Stand Out from the Competition	23
Personal Branding Allows You to Charge a Premium Price	26
Personal Branding Highlights Your Expertise	28
Personal Branding Allows You to Attract Your Ideal Audience	30
Personal Branding Puts You in Charge of the Narrative	32
Personal Branding Increases Your Visibility	34
Personal Branding Shapes What Content You Share	36
Personal Branding Connects You More with Individuals	38
Personal Branding Allows You to Become an Influencer	40
The Power of the Personal Brand	42
HOW TO BUILD A PERSONAL BRAND	44

Step #1: Determine Who You Really Are	44
Step #2: Determine What You Want to Accomplish	46
Step #3: Identify Your Target Audience	48
What's Possible – Client Success Story	51
Step #4: Determine Your Unique Value Proposition	52
Step #5: Start Treating Yourself as a Brand	56
Step #6: Create a Website and Automation System	58
Step #7: Develop Your Content Strategy	62
Step #8: Constantly Bring Your Best	66
Step #9: Build your Community (Online and locally)	68
Step 10: Get Seen, Heard	70
Step 11. Getting Paid	72
NOW IS THE TIME TO BUILD YOUR BRAND	73
ABOUT THE AUTHOR	76
RESOURCE PAGE	79

Introduction

Hey Mom! I am so glad you are here! Why? Because I know being a mompreneur is extremely challenging. You have been searching for the right resources and guidance to help you and your child build a successful business for a long time. I know because I've been exactly where you are. And after 10 years of helping my son, as well as countless others, achieve their business goals, I'm ready to share all my secrets with you. But first, let me introduce myself. I am Arriel Biggs, and I am what you call a Mom Boss. That is to say, I am a momager, business coach, youth entrepreneurship advocate, community organizer, master communicator, doting wife, head housekeeper, designated driver, and executive chef (I'm just playin. I'm really the boss of the 10 min quick meal)!

Like many of you, I want my kids to be prepared for living on their own. They need to know how to cook, properly clean, make money, and manage their finances without me. I want them to be successful in every way. I had a plan for how I was going to teach them all these things, only to be faced with cancer not even a couple months into our journey.

Yes, CANCER!!! And this would not be my first time battling this enemy. You can only imagine how crushed I was to hear that word again. It was like a ton of bricks hit me as I began thinking about the hardship of going through the fight and recovery process for a second time. What effect would it have on my children and my husband? Yet, nevertheless, my family and I bossed up and decided that we were going to WIN this battle ... TOGETHER! And we did!

So today, with even more passion and dedication, I am on a mission to help families win the battle against poverty and build generational wealth through entrepreneurship. I believe legacy, ownership, and financial freedom is a necessity for every family. I want to change the narrative of how we see ourselves, as well as how the world values our community of families. We are powerful, unstoppable, and determined. We are the real deal!

One of the ways I am helping families achieve their entrepreneurial goals is through my nonprofit organization Young Biz Kidz. Our mission is to empower young people all over the world by engaging and encouraging financial literacy and entrepreneurship. Financial education through entrepreneurship is a great way to introduce smart

money habits, effective communication, personal accountability, and problem-solving skills early.
I am also the founder and visionary behind YBK Day, a national youth marketplace held annually that teaches young entrepreneurs how to start and run a real business.

Initially, my focus was on just educating youth, but I soon realized that parents also needed guidance with helping their children build strong personal brands that carry influence. This led me to create a coaching program, *The Young Influencer Blueprint*, that equips parents with the necessary tools and information they need to help their children successfully attract customers, make more money, and have an indelible impact on their community. Let me say it again for the people in the back. We build businesses that make more MONEY and IMPACT our communities... period!

So, moms, today I am going to give you, my BLUEPRINT. I am providing you with the same steps I used to help my son build his personal brand and influence, which landed him a feature on B.E.T, his own official holiday, over 15,000 book sales, multiple speaking engagements, and the title of "Youngest Vending Machine Owner in the United States" according to Google!

I admit, I am bragging a bit as the list of accomplishments go on. But I share all of this to let you know that what was possible for Mikey can be possible for your young entrepreneur too.

So, grab a good reading spot, a cup of coffee, and your favorite notebook and let's get started on the journey to helping your child become a Young Influencer!

Who Is This Book Is For?

This book is not just for experienced Momagers,

It's for Moms that are thinking about getting into the youth entrepreneur space with their child.

It's for the Mom that has a child with a dream and not a dollar.

It's for the Mom that wants more for her child than what she had.

This book is for the Mom who wants to prepare her child/ren for the world of opportunity that waits before them.

I'm going to show you how I built a profitable personal brand with my child.

But Momma I need you to understand that you are important, valuable and that you matter too!
Your Strength to keep going even when it gets hard,

Your Courage to walk by faith,
Your Unwillingness to quit,

These are characteristics of a Phenomenal mom

This journey with my children allowed me to enjoy everyday life, gave me the freedom to celebrate small beginnings, and taught me to have mercy WITH MYSELF when I make a mistake as a mom and a momager.

I'm not only gaining success financially but also, I'm gaining success in my mindset, and body. I'm not working myself crazy, I'm working smart and most importantly I'm doing it as myself maintaining my morals and building a business from a healthy place with my children, that's my ultimate goal.

Welcome to the Young Influence Blueprint
I Am Arriel Biggs, Your Guide

Let's Get Started

You know what a brand is. McDonald's, Apple, Lexus, Nike, and Gucci are all brands.

But do you know what a personal brand is? And, even more importantly, do you know how to build one?

If you answered, "No," to either of those questions, then this book is for you.

Now, more than ever, you need a personal brand. If you want to stand out from the competition, attract new clients, and build a thriving business, it's important to create a powerful, thriving personal brand.

You see it's not just about your mission, it's also about how you carry it, and how you carry yourself. Anybody can be successful. We know this but not everybody knows how to handle success with a good character.

For example

Many of my son's opportunities came from people who fell in love with his authenticity, confidence, morals, and values. They would also tell us "how they loved how our entire family was a part of the business."

We have experienced all expenses paid opportunities: flights, transportation, food, hotel, and spending allowance per day. Not just for WHAT we brought to the table, but also for WHO we are at the table, we weren't perfect, and we didn't have all the answers but because of how we carried ourselves we gained access to things we could only dream of.

Many people that booked my son told me how relatable Mikey was to other kids.(he was being himself) He played video games, dressed like his peers, his style was like his peers and he faced some challenges in his life like his peers.

Okay Momagers, here's my moment to be transparent with you, we are from St. Louis, MO and at the time we lived in a rough area where violence and crime was right outside our front door. As a mom I saw my son had an entrepreneurial bug.

So this journey and building this business was very personal for me because the cars and the money had Mikey's attention and that wasn't a problem but his mindset on how to get those things was not clear.

A Lot of kids see the rappers, celebrities, and drug dealers & they believe that's the only way to get money. Usually the easiest way to get money is without character, self-respect, and morals and I AINT HAVING IT not then or now, I wanted the right thing in my son's hands before the wrong thing got into his hand.

Okay, back to the story

Most people thought my son was extremely smart and got straight A's in school. He is extremely intelligent but was a C student. My son struggled earlier on with writing and reading comprehension. So as you can imagine, writing a book was a big accomplishment for him; but making the bestseller list and selling over 15,000 copies of his children's book "Mikey Learns About Business" was the icing on the cake.

On the journey to building my son's personal brand and influence we shared the good, bad and ugly. I want to be clear, when we shared, we were ready to share we did not let anyone rush us to tell his story. We didn't let people push and pull us in direction; we didn't feel aligned with our morals and values.

Momager, hear me you **Do Not** have to share everything, somethings take time to share and you may never share them and it's OK. Keep this in your mind as you share, speak from a place where you feel safe and secure and what will help others; remember what comes from the heart reaches the heart. I know we are in a day and age where everything is put out on social media and people are doing anything to be seen even if it's detrimental to them, but I want you to understand that you are in control of your brand and story and how the world sees you & your young entrepreneur.

If you're an entrepreneur or a parent of a young entrepreneur, it's critical to devote at least some time each week to strengthening your brand. As you'll understand later, your personal brand is one of your biggest assets.

Your personal brand can take your business to places you never thought possible.

But you have to know how to build one.

Unfortunately, most business owners don't know how to build a personal brand. They feel fuzzy on exactly what steps to take and what's involved in creating a brand around themselves.

That's what this book is all about.

I'm going to give you a roadmap that will walk you through:

- What is a personal brand?
- Why you need a personal brand
- A step-by-step guide to building your own personal brand and influence

Ready?

Let's dive in.

What's Possible – Client Success Story

I'm Na-Tae', mom of Jahkil Jackson, founder of Project I Am & The Naeem Group. Before working with Arriel, I was all over the place, but with her guidance, I was able to organize and prioritize, ultimately creating a step-by-step plan for the success of my bestselling author son!

Jahkil crushed his 6-month book goal within 2 months, implemented an anti-bullying workshop to accompany his book, booked his first social entrepreneurship teaching series and even secured a written proclamation from the mayor for YBK Day to be an annual celebration of youth entrepreneurs!

After just one short year, Jahkil has been able to generate income from multiple avenues and has impacted thousands of youths nationally, all from one project. Can't wait for the next one!

What Is a Personal Brand?

First things first. Let's ensure we're all on the same page in terms of what a personal brand actually is.

A personal brand is much more than a flashy logo or a color palette. A personal brand goes far beyond having a nice-looking business card. A personal brand is not just about having a website with your name on it, although that's certainly part of it.

A personal brand is much bigger and all-encompassing. It's about who you are and what you do.

Your personal brand is how you present yourself, both online and offline, to your ideal audience.

Your personal brand is the image you put forth. It's what you stand for. Your values. What you're all about. The core of who you are as a person. Your personal brand is your secret sauce – the thing that sets you apart from everyone else. It's what makes you unique.

Your personal brand includes your:

- Values
- Unique skills
- Experiences
- Stories
- Personality
- Image

And each of these must be presented in an authentic, honest way to your audience.

Your personal brand centers around you as an individual. It's about what you bring to the table, the value that you offer. It involves the specific ways that you solve people's deepest pain points and biggest frustrations.

You may be tempted to think that only big companies are brands, but that's not true. Thanks to the internet and the power of social media, every person can be their own brand.

- Everyone can constantly put themselves out in front of their audience.
- Everyone can add value to their audience.
- Everyone can communicate their message loud and clear.

We all have the tools to build powerful personal brands.

In fact, you might say that every person is now a brand. The question is whether you are actively taking control of your brand.

As Influencer Marketing Hub puts it:

> You can either ignore your personal brand and let it develop organically, possibly chaotically, beyond your control, or you can help massage your personal brand to depict you as the person you want to be.

In other words, you're going to have a personal brand, whether you want to or not. Everything you share online, every email you send to your audience, every blog post you write, every live event you host - they all are part of your brand.

They all shape the way people think about you and the image your put forth.

The question is whether you want your brand to develop on its own, with no guidance from you, or whether you want to be actively in control of the process.

To state the obvious, it's always better when you're in control of the process.

So how do you actively build a personal brand? How do you get in control of the process? How do you ensure that your brand is helping to build your business?

That's what the rest of this book is about.

Why You Need to Build a Personal Brand

At this point, you might be thinking, Why do I need to build a personal brand? I'm not a big company. I'm not a Hollywood celebrity. Why do I need a brand?

Here's the reality: every entrepreneur, coach, consultant, freelancer, etc. should be building their own brand.

It doesn't matter if you're not a big name or a Fortune 500 company.

If you are trying to build a business of any sort, it's important to build your own personal brand. You don't need to be a large company or a Hollywood celebrity to benefit from building a personal brand.

Let's talk about some of the benefits of building a personal brand.

Personal Branding Allows You to Stand Out from the Competition

First and foremost, building a personal brand enables you to uniquely stand out from the competition.

Your brand, values, expertise, and story all set you apart from your competitors.

Your competitors can't bring what you bring to the table.

They simply don't have what you have to offer. You're unique. Only you are you.

You have unique:

- Experiences
- Strengths
- Beliefs
- Perspectives
- Skills
- Insights

...that set you apart from everyone else. These are incredibly valuable and distinguish you from your competitors.

You offer unique value that no other person can offer.

No one else can bring to the table what you can. No one else has your unique combination of skills, insights, and experiences.

Building your personal brand allows you to highlight your uniqueness.

It allows you to capitalize on your strengths. It allows you to highlight the best parts of you.

And as you work to highlight your strengths, it distinguishes you from all your competitors. It gives you a distinct competitive advantage.

Think about Rolex and how they've set themselves apart from the competition. Because they've focused on being exclusively a luxury watch brand, they have set themselves apart from other watch companies, like Timex.

Rolex is the brand for those who want a luxury watch, while Timex is the brand for those who want a sturdy, relatively inexpensive watch.

By working relentlessly to build their brand, Rolex has distinguished themselves from every other watch company.

The more you work to build your personal brand, the greater edge you'll have over your competition. You'll stand out amidst the crowd.

What's Possible – Client Success Story

Working with Mrs. Arriel really brought my idea of becoming an author to life! She helped me with my first self-published book and made it happen easily!

If anyone ever asks me how to do it, I will send them to Mrs. Arriel to experience the magic! She can literally make you an author in her sleep.

Thank you for your awesome work, Mrs. Arriel.

- Sidney Keys III founder of Books N Bros

Personal Branding Allows You to Charge a Premium Price

As noted, personal branding highlights just how unique you are and the incredible value that you offer.

Because you bring unique value to the table - value that no one else offers - you can charge a premium price for your services.

After all, you're offering something that can't be found anywhere else. Your services are only offered by you.

When you craft a strong personal brand, you can charge a higher price for your products and services because they're exclusive to you. They can't be purchased at another store or from another person.

The stronger your brand, the more people want your services. The more people want your services, the higher the price you can charge.

This is exactly why Nike can charge so much for their shoes. They've spent years building their brand into a powerhouse. Nike shoes have become a status symbol, and wearing Nikes says something about who you are.

This allows Nike to charge exorbitant amounts of money for their shoes. The Nike brand automatically equals higher prices for shoes.

You can take a page from Nike's book. By working hard to build your personal brand and showing how much value you bring to the table, you too can charge a premium price.

Personal Branding Highlights Your Expertise

Remember, your personal brand is how you present yourself to the world.

This means that a significant amount of personal branding involves the content that you share with the world.

The more valuable the content you share, the more you demonstrate that you're an expert who should be trusted.

With every piece of content that you share...

- Social media posts
- Blog posts
- Emails
- Videos
- Inspirational graphics
- Meditations
- Affirmations
- Audiobooks
- Podcasts

...you establish yourself as an expert in your field. As someone who really knows what they're talking about. As a thought leader in your arena.

You are demonstrating your knowledge and insight to the watching world. You're proving just how much value you offer and that you're the go-to person in your industry.

The more you demonstrate your expertise, the more your audience will trust you and come to you to solve their problems.

The more value you share, the more it shows people that you know exactly what you're talking about and should be looked at as an expert.

Personal Branding Allows You to Attract Your Ideal Audience

Being known as an expert in your field brings unique benefits with it.

When you're known as the expert in your industry:

- It attracts your ideal audience - the people who need your help the most.
- You get more referrals from others in your industry and related industries.
- You can charge a premium price - the kind of price that only an expert can charge.

Tony Robbins is a prime example of this. For years, he has been sharing the same message of self-empowerment.

Everything he says, every video he puts out, every book he writes has the same brand message: you can develop into a powerful individual, and I can help you to do that.

Over time, he has established himself as one of, if not the, go-to person in the self-development arena.

The results?

- He attracts huge audiences of people who want to fulfill their potential.
- Millions of people read his books and follow him on social media.
- He can charge a premium price for his services.

By consistently building his personal brand over many years, Tony Robbins now has people flocking to him for advice.

Do you want to experience the Tony Robbins effect?

If you want to be known as the go-to person in your industry, then it's absolutely essential that you begin building your personal brand as soon as possible.

Personal Branding Puts You in Charge of the Narrative

As I noted earlier, your personal brand will evolve, whether you want it to or not. If you:

- Use social media
- Have an email list
- Have a blog
- Speak to groups
- Record and share videos

...then you're already building your personal brand. Everything you put out into the world is part of your personal brand.

The question is whether you're intentionally shaping the narrative of your brand.

In other words, are you carefully determining exactly what your brand is all about, or are you letting it happen in an ad-hoc manner?

Are you thoughtfully curating your brand or are you letting your brand "evolve" on its own? Are you the one crafting people's opinions about your or are you sort of just letting things happen?

The beauty of personal branding is that it ensures that you're actively shaping your own narrative.

You're determining what others think about you, rather than simply letting them form their own opinions.

With every social media post you share, every blog post you put up, every email you send, you're shaping the narrative of who you are. You're in control of the story.

Personal Branding Increases Your Visibility

The more you build your personal brand, the more visible you'll become.

- You'll attract more fans on social media.
- Those fans will share your content with their tribes.
- The more your content gets shared, the more fans you'll attract.
- And repeat

It's a powerful cycle.

As your fan base grows, you can expect to be featured in the media.

Media outlets are always looking for experts to comment on particular subjects, and when you become known as the expert in your field, you'll start generating media requests. The more you're featured in media outlets, the more opportunities you'll have to speak in front of crowds. Conference organizers are always looking for well-known media personalities to speak.

The truth is, building your personal brand and building your platform go hand-in-hand.

As your personal brand grows stronger, your platform will get bigger, which will then make your brand stronger.

Building your brand is a virtuous cycle that brings greater and greater results the more you do it.

Personal Branding Shapes What Content You Share

If you don't have a strong personal brand, then you don't have any guidelines as to what content you should share with your audience.

And so you end up sharing either nothing at all or whatever catches your fancy at any given moment. Neither of these strategies contributes to your personal brand.

When you have a strong personal brand, it guides you toward exactly what kinds of content you should share.

Simply put, you should only share content that aligns with and promotes the values of your personal brand.

A meme might be funny, but if it doesn't add to your personal brand, you shouldn't share it.

What's Possible – Client Success Story

I'm Hilda, mom of Christianna Alexander, better known as "The Sweet Boss and the founder of Sweet Christi's.

Before working with Arriel we lacked strategy and only generated income from a few sources. After working with Arriel we were able to implement additional streams that required less work to maintain.

Christi was able to sell 500 books in just one day, became a bestselling author and secured a written proclamation from the mayor for YBK Day to be an annual celebration of youth entrepreneurs in Jacksonville Florida!

Arriel also helped Christi to partner with youth all over the world promoting youth entrepreneurship and kindness. Christi's brand has been elevated tremendously and still has room to grow with Arriel.

Personal Branding Connects You More with Individuals

The simple truth is people connect better with people than they do with companies. It's why Elon Musk and Richard Branson have more individual Twitter followers than the companies they founded.

The more you work to build your personal brand, the more individuals will want to connect with you, both in-person and online. People will be attracted to your values, personality, convictions, and the insights you have to offer.

The more connected you are, the more business opportunities will present themselves to you. More speaking requests. More media opportunities. The opportunity to partner with other like-minded people.

Building your personal brand connects you personally with potential customers and clients, which then builds your business.

Pia Silva puts it like this:

> "With so much content and so many small businesses popping up online, a brand that connects to a person's face is much easier to trust faster. It takes less time and effort to build a relationship with a personal brand as compared to a business brand."

Personal Branding Allows You to Become an Influencer

The more you develop your personal brand, the more you become known as an "influencer". An influencer is someone who significantly shapes the opinions of their followers and has a big influence on how they behave.

There are some significant benefits to being an influencer:

- Big brands want to work with influencers that have a large audience, which can result in more revenue for you.
- You often receive free things from companies who are interested in partnering with you.
- You receive media requests to speak at, or even just attend events.

If you want to get in on these perks, start working to develop your personal brand.

What's Possible – Client Success Story

"Arriel, thank you again for the Young Influencer Blueprint. Since we put the plan into action for my son's business "Rico's Rockin' Pop", requests from local businesses and organizations to work with him have been nonstop.

He has done interviews, book signings and received a proclamation from Clark County, NV for his work highlighting youth entrepreneurship. Your promotion strategies have made a huge impact on his business."

~ Jennifer Cruz Momager of Rico Cruz

Arriel is a gifted educator and mentor for youth entrepreneurship, as well as parents of young entrepreneurs.

She made the process of writing my daughter's brand book seamless. Not only did my daughter become a bestselling author, but under Arriel's guidance, she was able to grow her platform nationally over the course of just a few months!

~ Anissa Wright Momager of Jordyn Wright Best-Selling author of "The Clean Truth About Starting A Business for Teens"

The Power of the Personal Brand

Are you starting to see the power of your personal brand? Your personal brand is what enables you to distinguish yourself from the competition. It allows you to charge a premium price for your services.

The more you focus on your personal brand, the more visible you become, and the more you become known as the expert in your field. The more you're known as an expert, the more opportunities come your way.

And the more you build your personal brand, the more you connect with others, which in turn builds your business even more.

Kevin Stimpson says this:

> "Having a personal brand is important for an entrepreneur because now more than ever, it's important for CEOs and founders of companies/brands to come out to the forefront and connect with their audiences. People connect with people."

It's safe to say that there are few things more powerful than your personal brand. The more you focus on building it, the greater the results you'll see.

Now, are you ready to start building your personal brand?

How to Build a Personal Brand

Now that you know why you should build a personal brand, let's talk about how to actually do it. Let's break down the individual strategies you can use to build your own incredibly powerful personal brand.

Step #1:
Determine Who You Really Are

The first step in creating a powerful personal brand is to determine who you are. Remember, building your personal brand is about sharing your authentic self with the world.

Tyler Basu helpfully puts it like this:

> Your personal brand should not be an inauthentic persona. Branding is not about positioning yourself as something that you are not. It's about purposefully and strategically showcasing your authentic self to your audience and your customers. Your personal brand should be a true reflection of your skills, passions, values, and beliefs.

To put it another way, your personal brand is built upon your skills, passions, values, and beliefs. You must know yourself if you want to build a strong personal brand.

Ask yourself:

- What unique skills do I have?
- What are my core values?
- What am I most passionate about?
- What unique experiences have shaped who I am?
- How can I most effectively serve my core audience?
- What do I have to offer that no one else does?

The answers to these questions should shape your personal brand. They should help you get to the core of what matters most to you and how you can add value to your audience.

The Benefit- When your childcares about the mission/cause it makes it easier for them to run the business even when it's not all fun and games.

Action Steps
1. Do a brain dump of all the things your child is naturally good at.
2. Make a list of possible problems your child can solve with their skill sets.
3. Pick one idea and start planning

Step #2: Determine What You Want to Accomplish

Once you've identified the core of who you are, it's time to think about what you want to accomplish with your personal brand.

Answer these questions:

- What would I like to accomplish, both personally and professionally?
- What do I want to be known for?
- If I could be the world's foremost expert on a topic, what would it be?
- What key message do I want to communicate?
- If I could only give one piece of advice, what would it be?

The answers to these questions should further solidify in your mind what your personal brand will look like.

What's Possible – Client Success Story

I'm L. Michelle Woods-Starkes, mom of Gabrielle O. Starkes, CEO of GO! Bubbles.

Before working with Arriel, I believed I could map out Gabrielle's journey to launch her book and tie in her GO! Bubbles brand. I was wrong!

After working with Arriel we met our goals! I was able to gain clarity on what needed to be done step by step to allow Gabrielle's business to grow and make her a youth authority in her community. Work with Arriel!

~ L. Michelle Woods-Starkes

My name is Sharron. I am the mother of DeJuan Strickland, the author of Tech Boy. Working with Arriel has been amazing. She has guided me through my son's self-publishing journey.

From DeJuan's launch plan to his release; she has held my hand through this process. With her coaching DeJuan's presale goal was 50 and within 7 days he pre-sold 88 books. He Is now on his way to selling 1,000 copies of Tech Boy. We thank her for all the gems she has bestowed upon us.

~ Sharron Prather Momager of DeJuan Strickland

Step #3:
Identify Your Target Audience

The simple reality is that you can't effectively serve everyone. Rather, there is a core demographic of people who will resonate deeply with you, your brand, and what you offer.

This core demographic is your target audience. It's these people whom you will serve most effectively and who will be your ideal client.

To identify your core audience, ask yourself these questions:

- Who can I most effectively help?
- Who will benefit most from my skill set and knowledge?
- Who am I most passionate about serving?
- Who will resonate most with me and my brand?

When determining your core audience, it can be helpful to create a persona. This persona represents your ideal client. Include the following information in the persona:

- Demographics: How old are they? Male? Female? Single? Married? What is their level of education? What career are they in? How much do they make?

- Hopes and dreams: What do they want their future to look like? What are their goals?

- Challenges: What obstacles do they face? Why haven't they been able to reach their goals?

Kyle Gray says this about finding your ideal audience:

> "The foundation of a strong personal brand is how well you understand your audience and the problems they face. Then you can define why you care and how you solve those problems, which is what you'll be remembered for."

The Benefit- It makes it easier to talk to them because you are speaking the same language

Action Steps
1. Do your research
2. Create a consumer persona
3. Write out 10 of their pain points

What's Possible – Client Success Story

I'm Christianna Alexander, owner of the beauty brand Sweet Christi' and I worked with Mrs. Arriel Biggs to complete my new book Stay Sweet and Never Miss A Beat.

I loved the process from beginning to end. Before working with Mrs. Arriel I couldn't finish my book and sat on the project for some time.

Mrs. Arriel listened to everything I wanted and guided me through the process. The end result is a beautiful book that I'm proud of and it's super easy to promote because I love it so much.

Ms. Arriel made sure I enjoyed the process and celebrated each step, including hitting the publish button. I'm already looking to work on the next project with her.

Step #4:
Determine Your Unique Value Proposition

Now it's time to identify your Unique Service Proposition (USP).

Your USP is simply your brand summed up into a single, powerful compelling statement that describes exactly what you do for your audience.

It's where you take all the answers from the previous three points and put them together into one brand statement that sums up who you are personally and how you serve your core audience.

A USP typically looks something like this:

- I help (target person) to (achieve X) so that they can (outcome)

For example, your USP may be something like, "I help working moms stay on top of everything and live a fulfilled life."

Or, "I help entrepreneurs scale their businesses over six-figures per year so they can live a life of freedom."

Or, "I help men be incredibly productive so that they have more time to spend with their friends and families."

Your USP doesn't have to say everything about your brand, but it should get right to the heart of who you are and how you help your audience.

It may help to give your USP a unique name that will stick in people's mind. For example, if you teach men how to be more productive, you could call your USP the "Power Productivity Formula".

Or if you help entrepreneurs scale their businesses, you could call your USP something like, "Scale Without Fail."

You get the point. It simply needs to be short, memorable, and aptly describe what you do.

Avoid skimping on this step. Creating your USP gives you a high degree of clarity about what your brand is all about.

Take the necessary time to craft a USP that adequately captures what your brand is about.

The Benefit- once you understand what makes you different and how to communicate it to you audience it helps your consumer buying decision easier

Action Steps
1. Write out your child's I help statement follow this format (I help xyz _____ do xyz _____)
2. Understand the problem you are solving, and who it will benefit
3. Understand that you have a product that is geared to children, but the parent is spending the money

What's Possible – Client Success Story

Arriel is so amazing and enjoys what she does. She's positive, supportive, humble, and honest. Our first meeting was overwhelming and challenging, but If it doesn't challenge you, it won't change you.

After the first meeting my hustler mentality and confidence went from 40% to 100 %. She has a gift/talent that I have never seen before. She's able to hold a conversation, listen to business ideas, and she immediately had a solution or some feedback.

She has a way of motivating others and transferring her positive energy into them. She was calm and soft spoken, but her energy was loud and vigorous. I would put her in the category of a hype man lol.

I was able to gather ideas, clarify my vision, reform my daughters business, start brainstorming ideas for my own business, while learning how to manage my time wisely, and to start balancing my personal and business goals . I will highly recommend her

~ Lasha Moore Momager of Madison and Mariyah owners of Sister Sisters Sweets

Step #5:
Start Treating Yourself as a Brand

Once you've identified the core of your brand, as well as your target audience, it's time to start treating yourself as a brand.

What does this look like practically?

In every communication with your audience, whether a blog post, email, podcast, social media post, etc., you stay true to your brand message.

You constantly speak about the problems you solve, constantly encourage your audience, constantly voice the message of your brand.

Just like Nike wouldn't suddenly start talking about camping, so you must not go off brand with your communications. You constantly reinforce your Unique Service Proposition in everything you do.

It also means creating a strong, compelling website to serve as your home base for all your online activities (more on this in a minute).

It means creating a media page or media kit on your site for media inquiries.

It could mean not answering emails yourself, but having an assistant answer them (or answering them under a pseudonym).

Your goal is to portray yourself as a strong, compelling brand, not just a normal person. You have to treat yourself like you truly are: a powerful brand that has a powerful message.

The Benefit- I like the saying if you stay ready you don't need to get ready. Treating yourself like a brand will help people take your child seriously in their business.

Action Steps
1. Make sure your child has a professional headshot
2. Write out your child's bio and update it regularly
3. Create a speaker one sheet
4. Write out your child core brand story

Step #6:
Create a Website and Automation System

Now it's time to get into the nitty-gritty of optimizing your online presence so that it matches your brand. You're going to start with your website, since this functions as your "home base" of sorts. In other words, your website is one of the primary places people get to know who you are and what you do.

Your website also functions as one of the primary ways you turn visitors into paying clients, and it must be optimized for that.

First impressions are really important when it comes to your website. Visitors should be able to immediately determine how you can help solve their problems. If they can't, there's a good chance they'll leave.

So how do you optimize your site to reflect your brand?

- Have a professional logo designed. Having a professional logo shows people that you're serious about what you do and really do treat yourself as a brand. If you wish to hire someone to design a logo for you, Fiverr and Upwork are great places to start.

- Show off your Unique Service Proposition. From the moment they arrive on your website, visitors should see your USP. It's what will draw them into your site and make them want to investigate more.

  Ideally, your USP will be front and center at the top of your website so that it's likely to be the first thing that people see. It should be impossible to miss. It should function like the main headline on a newspaper. The eye should be drawn to it immediately.

- Use professional photographs. Have a professional photographer take high-quality photos of you. Low-quality photos will ultimately reflect poorly on your brand.

- Use testimonials. Testimonials are proof that you really can solve people's problems. They help overcome your prospects' hesitance and objections. Also, if you've been featured in any media outlets, show off those credentials too.

- Present a clear call-to-action. Ultimately, you want people to take action when they're on your website. You want them to join your email list, watch your webinar, or sign up for a free consultation. Give visitors a clear call-to-action.

- Create a compelling "About" page. On your about, tell your story. How did you get to where you currently are? What motivates you to serve your audience? Why do you do what you do?

- Create a services page. If you want clients to hire you, it's important to have a clear services page in which you explain what you offer, what's included, and more.

- Give away free resources. One of the best ways to build your brand is to give away free content on your website. This could be anything from blog posts to videos to an eBook.

  Giving away content in exchange for a visitor's email address is also a fantastic way to grow your email list.

- Create a contact page. Obviously, you want a way for people to be in touch with you. This will happen primarily through your contact page on your website.

The Benefit-having a website is a great way to push traffic to a platform you own. It also allows you to put your supporters in a system that will capture information to market to them over time.

Action Steps
1. Buy a domain that is relatable to your brand
2. Create a website
3. Get an email marketing system
4. Create a lead magnet to get people to opt-in to your list
5. Send emails regularly and consistently

Step #7:
Develop Your Content Strategy

The primary way to build your brand is by creating strategic content. By content, we mean blog posts, videos, social media posts, emails, affirmations, podcasts, and more.

Every piece of content you share with your audience should serve to build your brand. As we mentioned before, once you've determined your brand, it's important to start treating yourself as a brand.

Developing a strategic content strategy is one of the most effective ways to ensure that you're constantly staying on brand.

When it comes to your content strategy, we recommend the "Pillar Method" (a term coined by Gary Vaynerchuk).

The Pillar Method works as follows:

- At set intervals (every day, every week, etc.) create a longer piece of "pillar" content. This could be a blog post, video, eBook, etc. The point is that it needs to be on the longer side so that it can be repurposed in numerous ways.

    This pillar content should always reinforce some part of your brand. Maybe one day you speak to a particular pain point. Another day you encourage your audience to strive for their goals. Whatever the case, it's essential that your pillar content always be tied back to your brand.

- Publish your pillar content on your primary platform, whether that's your blog, YouTube, iTunes, etc.

- Take your pillar content and cut it up into smaller, shareable pieces of content. In other words, if you have a 10-minute video, find three parts of that video that could be shared on their own and extract those clips.

If you have a 1,000-word blog post, extract five 100-word excerpts that can stand on their own.

- Share the smaller pieces of content across all your channels. Once you've created your smaller pieces of content, you're going to post those across all your channels, including Facebook, Instagram, LinkedIn, Twitter, email, etc.

    If the thought of posting to so many social media channels intimidate you, Buffer is a great tool that allows you to share to all your social media at one time. You just put the content in and then select all the channels you want it to go out to.

- Repeat the process again and again. Consistency is the key. By consistently sharing your brand message, you'll steadily build your audience.

By using the "Pillar Method" for your content strategy, you ensure that every piece of content you post is always on brand. Your Facebook posts, Instagram videos, blog posts, YouTube videos, and emails always are speaking your brand message to your audience.

In addition to using the "Pillar Method", you can also simply repurpose content into different formats. For example, you can turn an eBook into a SlideShare presentation or a series of blog posts into an eBook. Or you could turn a blog post into an email you send out to your list.

The main point is that everything you send out should be brand related. You want to constantly reinforce your brand to your audience.

The Benefit- with everything on your plate as a parent having a content strategy will help you with a plan to keep everything organized and in order.

Action Steps
1. Document everything you do (Write it down or record it)
2. Take Behind the scenes photos
3. Post on the platform where your audience is and put out valuable content

Step #8:
Constantly Bring Your Best

When it comes to building your brand, it's essential that you constantly give value to your audience without asking for anything in return. Yes, there will be times when you invite people to buy from you or become a client, but you don't want that to be the main theme of your brand.

The main thing people should take away when interacting with your brand is how much value you provide.

The main way you provide value is through your content strategy. Therefore it's so critical to constantly put out new content.

If you're not putting out new content, you're not giving away value.

Mark Lack puts it this way:

> "A strong personal brand is one that has a high level of impact, which then leads to influence amongst the people who follow you. The key is to leverage social media and other social platforms and environments to create relevant and meaningful dialogues between you and the people you want to impact."

The Benefit- This is simple, your child is at his/her best when they can be themselves

Action Steps
1. Allow your child freedom of creating their own style
2. If the energy is low in the room be the energy in the room
3. Allow your child to speak from their heart

Step #9:
Build your Community (Online and locally)

One of the best ways to build your brand is to build a community where you and the members can all help each other. The value in building a community around your brand is that it gets others involved in helping to promote your brand.

You create a tribe of passionate people who care about the same things you do.

So how can you build a community?

Some simple ways to build a community include:

- Start a private Facebook group. In this group, people can interact with each other, share ideas, interact with you, raise questions, etc.

- Host live events. Live events allow you to meet members of your tribe in person. Coffee meetups, retreats, workshops, masterminds, and private dinners are all great ways to deepen your relationships with them.

- Create a membership site. For a small monthly fee, you can give people exclusive access to you and the content you provide. You can also give them access to things like group calls every month, ongoing webinars, and a forum where they can interact with you and other members.

The Benefit-It allows you to have a village of support that is invested in your child's growth

Action Steps
1. Find a mentor in their industry (not all mentors are free)
2. Look to see who or what organization your child can serve in the community (through partnerships and collaborations)
3. Build your own community online or in your community.

Step 10: Getting Seen And Heard

The importance of getting seen and heard is to bring awareness to your child's brand and make money if your business systems are in place (but we will talk about that next step getting paid) Remember that your child's point of view and perspective matters. Have your child practice telling their story and let them know that each time they tell it have the same energy as the first time. Let your child know that this is the first time that audience is hearing your story. Getting seen and heard is a great way to start getting to support and building trust with your community.

The Benefit- It gives your audience a chance to connect with your child on a different level. It also allows you to get in front of new audiences.

Action Steps
1.Look for 3 podcast that align with your child brand.
2.Find 3 magazine source and email them your speaker one sheet (blogs work too)
3. Look for local radio interviews.
4. create your own show and invite quest to your platform.
Bonus step: If you have an event scheduled send press release to media outlets

What's Possible – Client Success Story

When I wrote on my 2020 goal list that I wanted to write a book I never imagined that so much would happen from it.

Mrs. Arriel helped me through the whole process, and it was so easy and fun! I wrote the book with the hopes of helping younger kids deal with being bullied and helping them to love and appreciate themselves.

Within 1 month I was a best-seller and had met my book sale goal 4 months early by selling 1,100 books within 2 months. From there I added an anti-bullying workshop for kids where I was able to interact with kids from across the country, reading my book to them and engaging them around self-worth and standing up for what's right.

I also became the Chicago ambassador for YBK Day, an initiative I plan to lead every July for kidpreneurs! Thank you, Mrs. Arriel!

Jahkil Jackson, founder of Project I Am & The Naeem Group.

Step 11. Getting Paid

There is a ton of ways to get paid when you are getting seen and heard. You can charge a fee for appearances and speaking. Some other examples are hosting a masterclass, affiliate programs, become a paid brand ambassador, workshops, conference or summit and my personal favorite writing a book.

The Benefit- Writing a brand book gives you instant authority, creates additional income streams and it's a way to pass down generational wealth. Examples of other income streams from creating a brand book: Workshops, Bootcamps, Conference and Masterclass

Action Steps:
For writing a Brand Book
1. Make a Writing Plan
2. Have your child write out their journey
3. Edit
3. Decide layout and formatting
4. Buy ISBN
5. Hire an illustrator
6. Design marketing items
7. Plan Launch
8. Start Pre-Sales
9. Launch Party

Now Is the Time to Build Your Brand

The simple truth is, you have a personal brand, whether you want to or not. Every single thing you share with your audience either adds to or takes away from your personal brand. You absolutely must be intentional about building your brand.

As Kathy Klotz-Guest says, "We all have a personal brand whether we think about it that way or not. So, let's be intentional about it."

Thankfully, it's not particularly difficult to build a personal brand.

Here's a quick summary of what we covered:

- Identify what matters to you.
- Define your core audience.
- Determine your Unique Service Proposition.
- Treat yourself like a brand.
- Create a website and automation system
- Create your content strategy.
- Constantly bring your best self to your audience.
- Build your community
- Get Seen and Heard.
- Get Paid.

The more you do those things, the more you'll build your brand and the more you'll attract an audience of raving supporters.

Avoid waiting any longer to build your child's personal brand. Get started on it today! Your audience needs you. Get out there and start serving them. You'll be glad you did!

What's Possible – Client Success Story

Mom Bosses! I need to take this time to share a testimonial with you about my experience working with "THE" Arriel Biggs.

She has been a Godsend and one of the greatest assets to my son's business journey. Her insight and quick-thinking is out-of-this world. Her experience with giving you a clear road map to follow has been so impactful.

She's a natural, genuine, and so easy to work with. She knows her stuff and won't lead you wrong. I'm so glad God allowed our paths to cross. He led me to a genius when I least expected it and I'm so glad He did.

She has SO much knowledge, there's not much you can bring to her that she doesn't know how to tackle! #TheArrielBiggs #TheRealMomBoss

~ Queenie Jenkins Momager of Jabez & Christopher Jenkins owners of Kings & Gents Accessories

Dedication

This book is dedicated to my wonderful husband James Biggs, my beautiful children Mikey Wren and Ariel (AJ) Biggs.

Without them none of this would be possible. They are my inspiration and motivation. They're love is LITERALLY healing to me.

Thanks a ton!!!

Arriel "The Mom Boss" Biggs!

About The Author

Arriel Biggs
Entrepreneur, Author and Speaker

Arriel is a two-time cancer survivor and the founder of Young Biz Kidz and YBK Day, a nonprofit organization whose mission is to empower young people by engaging and encouraging financial literacy and entrepreneurship in youth. She believes that teaching financial education through entrepreneurship is a great way to introduce smart money habits early.

In addition to providing income, Arriel wants all to know that entrepreneurship teaches effective communication, personal responsibilities, and problem-solving skills. It also builds self-esteem and strong relationships making it a great resource economically, academically, and socially.

Initially focusing on educating youth, Arriel soon realized that parents could also use guidance in helping their children become business owners. She now offers services to educate, empower and equip parents with the self-confidence to support their kid entrepreneur with her Young Influencer Blueprint program for Momagers and their young entrepreneurs.

Always on the go, Arriel is a mentor, child advocate, parent advisor, public speaker. She has received many accolades for being a phenomenal woman entrepreneur and has been requested to share her knowledge with local, national, and international audiences.

Arriel has taken her role as Mom Boss to another level and began empowering moms and families to become the boss in their lives.

Resource Page

Websites

Grab your FREE Momager Resource Kit Here: www.younginfluencerblueprint.com/freekit

Sales Funnel & Website Builder: www.DigitalEmpireBuilder.com

Score: www.score.org/resources-young-entrepreneurs

SBA: www.youth.gov/federal-links/sba-small-business-administration-young-entrepreneurs

Young Biz Kid: www.YBKDay.org

www.Canva.com

Inshot – Video & Image Editor

Facebook Business Suite – Post Scheduler

Domain: Godaddy, Host Gator

Email list: Mail Chimps, Mailerlite

Business Address: P.O. Box, Ipostal

Electronic payment: Square, Paypal, Stripe

Website: Wix, Weebly, Shopify

Drop shipping: Tee Spring, Amazon

Print Marketing items: Vistaprint, 4imprint, Stickers Banners

Live Streaming platforms: Zoom, Streamyard, BeLive

Project management software: Trello, Asana

Schedule software: Calendly, Schedule Once

www.ingramcontent.com/pod-product-compliance
Lightning Source LLC
Chambersburg PA
CBHW051948160426
43198CB00013B/2354